MY CRAZY DREAMS

AMY PENNINGTON BRUDNICKI

BRUDNICKI-PENN PUBLISHING

Copyright © 2020 by Amy Pennington Brudnicki

All rights reserved.

No part of this book may be reproduced in any form or by any electronic or mechanical means, including information storage and retrieval systems, without written permission from the author, except for the use of brief quotations in a book review.

DEDICATION

To my Aunt Meff, who has encouraged me for years to make a book out of my dreams, this is for you. I hope you enjoy this big stack of crazy. I love you.

~ Amy

DEDICATION TO MY CELEBRITY SOULMATES

To my first loves, Bo Duke & Jon Bon Jovi, y'all missed out on a good woman, as is evident in this book. Or maybe you dodged a bullet—I guess it depends on how you look at it.

~Amy

CONTENTS

1

THE ART OF DREAMING

DREAMS. We all have them, or so they say. Some of us remember them, others do not.

It's somewhat bizarre to me that people don't remember their dreams, being that my own dream world has always been exceedingly active. Some would say that I remember mine solely because I keep a dream journal. That's simply not the case, though. I mean, it's true that I keep a journal of my more colorful dreams, but I've only started doing that in the past few years—and only because my dreams are usually absolutely bonkers.

I've just always remembered my dreams since I was quite young. I remember dreams that I had as a child, as a teenager, and as a young adult—some were nightmares, others were mediocre, others still were quite nice.

SO I CAN'T SAY WHY WE REMEMBER SOME DREAMS OVER OTHERS.

IN MY RESEARCH, I'VE LEARNED THAT WHEN YOU HAVE VIVID DREAMS, you're in REM sleep. During REM sleep—Rapid Eye Movement—your eyes move back and forth, rapidly, as the definition implies.

ALRIGHTY THEN. I'M COUNTING *THAT* AS EXERCISE!

I'M OFFICIALLY DEVELOPING THE FITBIT EYE MASK. OK, THAT'S A LIE. But if anyone in this *world* would try to make that a thing, it's me.

MOUNTAIN FOLKLORE HAS SOMETHING TO SAY ABOUT REPEATING dreams—something that my Appalachian ancestors failed me on.

According to legend, dreams are never to be told before breakfast if they're bad and never at all if they're good.

Superstition suggests that the retelling of a good dream will prevent it from ever coming to pass, and the telling of a bad dream will invite evil into existence.

THAT TOTALLY EXPLAINS WHY I NEVER MARRIED JON BON JOVI AND WHY a dark cloud of calamity sometimes follows me. No one ever told me to keep my trap shut.

I've always repeated my dreams the second my feet hit the floor because they have always been absolutely looney.

As a matter of fact, when I was a teenager, I used to tell Mom all about that craziness. After a string of particularly disturbing dreams, she told me if I kept having them, she was taking me to see someone.

I might've been from the holler, but I knew what that meant.

THAT WAS THEN, AND THIS IS NOW.

. . .

If y'all don't hear from me again, she's taken me to see someone this time, and they've kept me.

If that Fitbit Eye Mask hits the market, someone speak up for me, and tell people that I invented it first.

Now that I've explained a little about my dream process, about Appalachian Folklore and why my last name is Brudnicki and not Bon Jovi, without further ado, I give you *My Crazy Dreams . . .*

I hope you enjoy this flaming hot mess.

2

RAMSAY

January 1999

When I was pregnant with Tyler, I dreamed that Bru ran off with the baby after I had him and named him without asking me. I dreamed he named him Ramsay.

After I had him—for real—the pediatrician came in and introduced himself as Dr. Ramsay.

What made this especially funny was that I only knew the name of one doctor in the practice, and Ramsay was not it.

3

ROOSTER & RABBIT

OCTOBER 22, 2009

LAST NIGHT I DREAMT THAT A ROOSTER AND A RABBIT WERE IN harnesses like you would put a dog in. No one in my dream thought this was odd at all.

4

SONYA RICHARDSON FIRED ME

FEBRUARY 16, 2010

I DREAMED THAT SWEET LITTLE SONYA RICHARDSON FIRED JAMIE, Penny, and me from a preschool job/cafe job.

I tried to reapply, and sweet little Sonya Richardson said that I was the dullest person *ever* and wouldn't re-hire me.

5

COFFEE

February 18, 2010

I dreamed I spent $502 dollars on a cup of coffee at Star Bucks.

That was a nightmare and a half.

(1) I spent $502 on coffee.
(2) It was coffee.

6

CREEPY CRAWLIES & WEBSITES

JULY 06, 2010

MY SWEET DREAMS WENT LIKE THIS: I DREAMED WE WERE HELPING A friend paint her *haunted* house. She let a giant, white anaconda snake loose—and I stayed!

There was a *giant* bullfrog that would blow out his lip. It would touch my leg, and I would scream thinking it was the snake.

THEN I DREAMED THAT BUB, KIM, AND I WERE ON THE PEOPLE OF WAL-Mart website, and my neighbor tagged us so everyone would know who we were.

FUN TIMES . . .

7

TERI COLLINS, MY CHILD

July 13, 2010 - recalling a 1980s dream . . .

To Teri Collins: Did I ever tell you when we were teenagers that I dreamed you were a minister?

I remember that dream, clearly, still today—which is amazing 'cause I can't remember anything.

I dreamed we were in the middle bedroom of my house, and you and I were sitting on the twin bed. I was crying over some boy.

You kept putting your hands on my shoulder and calling me, "My child." You kept saying everything was going to be ok.

It was never mentioned, but just understood that you were a minister.

8

FORKS' CHURCH PARTY

AUGUST 10, 2010

TO FRAN FORD: I DREAMED THAT YOU, DANIELLE LEWIS, KIM, BOOSE, me, and a bunch of other people were having a party in the church near Napier Florist.

I suppose we all came home for the Mary Breckinridge Festival after all.

PARTYING IN A CHURCH . . . YEP, THAT'S ABOUT AS WILD AS I GET.

9

MAYBE YOU CAN TAKE IT WITH YOU

SEPTEMBER 06, 2010

I DREAMED I SAW A HEARSE TRAVELING ON A WINDY DIRT ROAD. IT WAS only the hearse with no cars following it.

What was following it was a small storage trailer hooked to the hitch. Guess someone was taking their stuff with them, after all.

10

VOTE FOR EUGENIA STEWART

June 24, 2011

To Eugenia Stewart: I dreamed about you last night.

I dreamt that you were running for office. Your way of assuring votes was giving people old pictures of their family.

I really loved mine.

You got my vote.

11

SUSAN WILLIAMS & THE VINTAGE DOODADS

July 11, 2011

To Susan Williams: I dreamed about you last night.

I dreamed we went back and visited a house that you lived in as a child.

No such house ever existed; you know how dreams go.

There was an aquarium, a typewriter, an old china cabinet . . . All these things seemed to make us so happy.

12

WART FOOT

August 26, 2011

The other night, I dreamed that my little neighbor girl had two warts on her foot.

I dreamed that her Mom, Dad, and I were chasing the bus. I suppose we were gonna drag her off the bus and treat her!

No one goes down on my watch.

Or something like that.

13

SPIDER SLAYERS

SEPTEMBER 21, 2011

TO TERRY NORTH: I DREAMED THAT RUTH AND I SQUISHED A SPIDER AS big as a hamster, then we called ourselves the Spider Slayers.

YOU'RE A PSYCHIATRIC DOCTOR—OR SOMETHING IN THAT FIELD. I'M sure this book will keep you quite busy analyzing me.

14

IF Y'ALL ARE HERE UNDER THE MISCONCEPTION THAT WE'LL FEED YOU, YOU'RE SADLY MISINFORMED

OCTOBER 15, 2011

TO MY SISTER, KIM: I HAD THE MOST *INSANE* DREAM ABOUT US.

YOU AND I HAD INVITED ALL THESE PEOPLE OVER—THAT WE DIDN'T know—for a cookout.

At one point, I looked around and said, "If you all are here under the misconception that we'll feed you, you've been sadly misinformed. We forgot to buy food."

The rest of the dream involved taking out the trash, mowing grass, and manhandling a water hose—I guess in preparation for a cookout.

STILL YET, THERE WERE OTHER EVENTS IN THE DREAM. THERE WAS A flood, driving backwards at high speeds, Tyler being *extremely* rude to someone on the phone, an unexpected wedding reception for Uncle

Eddie—which we took all the partygoers to that weren't offended by my blunt remark—someone smoking in our house, one of the partygoers, I assume . . .

NEEDLESS TO SAY, I WOKE UP *ILL*RESTED WITH A *RAGING* HEADACHE FROM my weird, restless dream.

15

THIS IS MY BABY, SO AND SO

October 24, 2011

I dreamed that I had a baby girl—like, walked into the room, and, *hello,* there's a child.

I had no memory of having her, when her birthday was, *or* what her name was.

I dreamed I showed her to Mammaw and said, "Mammaw, look at my baby, Kade."

Bru says, "That's not what we named her!"

So I was calling her Kade—a nickname—with no memory of what her actual name was.

16

LAURA & AMI, THE MEAN GIRLS

December 03, 2011

To Laura Thomas: I dreamed about you and Amy Garner Hotchkiss last night.

I dreamed that you guys were at my house—but you know how dreams go, it was a place I have never seen before.

Anyway, I looked around and had an OMG moment. My house was tore upside down—as in frat boy party mess.

I was horrified. I kept saying, "I don't know what happened! My house *never* looks like this."

Amy said, "Well, it's looked like this *every time* I've ever been here!"

I also dreamed that she spelled her name "Ami," and everyone but me was aware of it. She was pretty upset that I didn't even know how to spell her name.

. . .

Needless to say, I was pretty happy to wake up and get away from you mean girls.

17

RENEE GRANT, BLAKE SHELTON & THE MYSTERY

OCTOBER 29, 2012

TO RENEE GRANT: SO LAST NIGHT, I DREAMED THAT WE WERE IN SMALL group together. You were out of town, and Alecia was doling out gifts on your behalf.

They were a cross between a three foot stuffed giraffe and Peanut from Jeff Dunham's skit.

I got sidetracked on the reason for the gifts because I was distracted. I kept staring at our newest member thinking, "Blake Shelton, why are you here? Blake Shelton, you're kinda beautiful . . ."

ANYWAY, IT GOT TO MY TURN FOR A GIFT. ALECIA TURNED TO ME AND smiled. As she was passing my green and purple stuffed animal to me, she said, "Mom wants you to know-"

THE ALARM WENT OFF BEFORE SHE COULD FINISH.

. . .

Darn you, Blake Shelton.

18

ME, THE DOG, KIM & THE GREAT EGG ROUNDUP

JANUARY 12, 2013

TO JENNIFER ASHER: I DREAMED I WAS AT YOUR HOUSE—WHICH LOOKS nothing like your house.

I was talking . . . to your dog. Not only that, but it was talking back and asked me to pray for it. At no time in the conversation did it strike me as odd that I was talking *with* a dog.

I ALSO DREAMED THAT KIM AND I WERE TRYING TO ROUND UP SOME OF her eggs so I could have a baby. Where her eggs went, I don't know. And why we couldn't use mine, I'm not sure.

HOWEVER, I DID CONVERSE WITH DOGS . . . SO MAYBE WE WERE AFRAID of the youngin' I'd manage to produce.

NEEDLESS TO SAY, I WOKE UP PRETTY DAGGONE WORE OUT.

19

CHERYL PARDINGTON & THE BOOK BLING

February 25, 2013

To Cheryl Pardington: I dreamed about your book bling last night.

I dreamed I was in Massachusetts researching the area for my book. I was in the hallway of a high-rise office building. When I turned the corner, I found myself roaming the halls of this super creepy hospital—because that's how I roll in my dreams.

When I came to a waiting room, I thumbed through the magazines they had and found five of your fabric bookmarks—one of them was purple. I was so excited.

I scooped them up, took a picture, captioned it, "SQUEE," and texted it to you.

How is it that I can remember details like this, but yet when I go to the store, I can't remember half of what we need?

20

ERIN JOHNSTON, BLAKE SHELTON & THE PEDICURE

June 16, 2013

To Erin Johnston: I dreamed that Blake Shelton gave me a pedicure. I have no idea how he did, though. Didn't look at my feet once.

21

DREAMING OUT LOUD

JUNE 26, 2013

WOKE UP WITH MY PHONE IN MY HAND. SO IF I CALLED YOU AND TALKED about James Patterson's quirky hospitality, Erin's Blake Shelton addiction, or the fact that I liked my mother's multi-color ink pen that she had when I was little, do not be alarmed.

I WAS JUST DREAMING OUT LOUD...

22

CASSIE GREEN BRADLEY & THE VOLKSWAGEN BEETLE ROLLERCOASTER, JAMIE LOVELL & THE AUCTION, BOOSE'S DOGS & ME

August 04, 2013

Last night, I dreamed that Cassie Green Bradley and I went to King's Island. We didn't buy tickets, so we decided to drive her Volkswagen Beetle around the rollercoaster tracks.

Not once did either of us question that decision.

Then the dream turned to auctioning stuff off with Jamie Lovell that I don't think belonged to either of us.

The scene changed again and eventually ended with me chasing two of Boose's dogs down to give them a bath—which I did a poor, poor job of because they would go opposite directions.

Geez. And that's why I'll be taking a nap today—not that I need an excuse, but that's why.

23

MARY ANN, BOOSE, ME, HOMEWORK & THE HIT

August 25, 2013

I love Sunday naps . . .

I dreamed that my cousin, Boose, and I were trying to help my neighbor, Mary Ann Sowers, with homework.

We were studying flash cards. The word was "Italy," and we were all struggling.

Mary Ann brought out pie, then it was all good.

She was also trying to arrange a hit on a guy who lived by a gambling establishment.

Again, there was dessert, so we were completely on board.

24

JO ANN LEWIS' HOUSE, THE BURGLAR & MY CAR

NOVEMBER 08, 2013

I HAD AN UNINTENTIONAL NAP THIS EVENING THAT CAUSED ME TO WAKE up laughing. In the dream, I was driving down the road on Hurricane Creek when I saw a guy breaking into a house.

It made me so mad that I ran him over. I don't know how I got inside this split foyer house where Jo Ann and David used to live—or why my car fit—but I aimed it at the steps and ran his sorry butt over . . .then drove right on out the front door.

25

ANYONE NEED A BABYSITTER?

December 23, 2013

Last night, I dreamed that Bru and I had another baby. We were staying in a motel and got the baby its own room so we could sleep.

Clearly, this means we're good with kids. Who needs a babysitter?

26

CHERYL PARDINGTON & THE CONVENTION CENTER

March 14, 2014

To Cheryl Pardington: I dreamed I was at a convention center in Chicago. I was all alone and had no idea why I was there. I was so relieved when you found me because you were the only one I knew.

We were chatting it up about books and Tracy when they shushed us.

Harrumph… How rude.

We were just about to find out why we had been brought there, then I woke up. Grrr.

27

GET IN THEM PANTYHOSE, DONKEY

March 21, 2014

Dear Lord! I dreamed I was attempting to put pantyhose on a donkey because my little Mammaw said we were keeping him.

He was kicking his legs every which way and not too willing.

I'm wore the heck out.

28

KITTY & THE BABY ELEPHANTS

May 11, 2014

I dreamed our dog—we have a cat—was giving birth to baby elephants. Yeah. So that's how my Mother's Day started.

Moral to this story? When life hands you baby elephants, you just roll with it . . .

29

CARRIE CALHOUN, TRUE BLOOD & PESKY KIN

June 22, 2014

To Carrie Calhoun: I dreamed about you last night. I dreamed you were an actress on True Blood, and I was pumping you for information to see if Alcide would have a lot of air time for tonight's premiere.

You weren't helpful . . . at all.

That's no way to treat your cousin.

30

KIM MOSES & THE NOISY ROOMMATE

June 23, 2014

To Kim Moses: I dreamed about you last night.

I dreamed we were on vacation and asleep in a motel. My stomach kept growling.

For a long time.

You finally raised up, looked over at me, and told me to eat something already because my stomach was keeping you awake.

Acting like a Pennington, girl.

31

NICOLE NEELEY, ME & THE AQUA NET

October 12, 2014

To Nicole Neeley: I dreamed that we were aqua netting our hair. We had it jacked up to Jesus. Then, we flipped each side over the front of our shoulders, leaving only about an inch wide strip visible from behind.

Just like days of old . . .

32

JAMIE BRANDENBURG, ME & MY DOCTORING

January 24, 2015

To Jamie Brandenburg: Last night, I dreamed I was running a clinic. It was in a warehouse. A pretty vacant warehouse, at that.

You were my first patient/victim. Once you came into the exam room, it occurred to me—for the first time—that I didn't know the first thing about doctoring someone.

But that didn't stop me.

I had you step up on the scale, which was actually a treadmill. I guess I was expecting an influx of people because I began multitasking. I made you take your temperature while you were on the "scale." The thermometer was attached to the wall with a cord, like those kinky-curly phone cords of yesteryear.

. . .

Anyway, I woke up before you ran away.
So, I hope this finds you well.

33

UNCLE DAVE & THE WALKING TACOS

January 27, 2015

To Uncle Dave: I dreamed I came to your house to make you potato soup. Instead of eating that, we had walking tacos—which is all the fixin's for tacos, you just eat it in a bag of Fritos instead of a taco shell.

So, if I were a dream analyzer, I'd just say I went to bed hungry.

(February 2020 Note: My Uncle Dave has since left this earth. God rest his soul. The day that I was editing this dream—nearly five years later—we were planning Walking Tacos for supper that night. For that menu and the editing of this dream to come together on the same day, I just felt like that was Uncle Dave's way of sending a little message to say hello.)

34

JOHNNY PAUL & THE RIGHT PROPER DUSTING

FEBRUARY 06, 2015

TO JOHNNY PAUL: I DREAMED YOU TOLD ME WE WERE GETTING twenty-five inches of snow. I was so excited.

THERE'S SOMETHING WRONG WITH ME.

35

DAWN BRUMFIELD, ME & THE GORILLA

March 08, 2015

To Dawn Brumfield: I dreamed we were in Kroger. I was trying to decide what I'd spent $179 on.

I had bread, bananas, and an Amazon card.

You walked into the store with this little tiny woman. You were talking to her about a gorilla when you came up to me to say hi. I looked at her and mouthed, "That's me," and pointed to myself. She looked horrified, but we thought that was hilarious.

So there you have it. My shenanigans extend into my dreamland.

36

BRENDA ROBINSON & THE TALL CAR

MARCH 13, 2015

TO BRENDA ROBINSON: I DREAMED ABOUT YOU LAST NIGHT.

I DREAMED YOU HAD A NEW CAR. IT WAS GUNMETAL GRAY AND BOXY AS all get out. When I opened the door, I realized why it was so tall—you stood up to drive.

37

LESLIE PASLEY, AMANDA SMITH, TRACY CRUSE, AND AMY COLLINS

March 22, 2015

To Leslie Pasley: Well, I dreamed about you and the girls last night. There was a big mob of us. We entered a competition. The gist was that we would build something out of everyday materials.

Once we entered the building, they split our groups. You, me, Amanda, Tracy, and Amy C. went to one group, everyone else was sent across the arena to their group.

They made a bow—as in, bow and arrow—out of strips of cloth and ketchup. It was as big as a harp!

You, all on your own, made not one, but two guitars. I have no idea what you used. They were the most beautiful things I ever laid eyes on.

. . .

I ACTUALLY CRIED.

I DON'T KNOW WHO WON, BUT YOU GAVE ME A GUITAR. I COULDN'T WAIT to get home and Facebook a picture of my beautiful handmade guitar. And since I can't do that, you're stuck with this story.

38

BOOSE, ME & HAWAII

July 27, 2015

To Boose: I dreamed about you.

We worked *all* night trying to get to Hawaii. We never made it, and now I'm too tired to go.

39

BOOSE, ME & THOSE 1980S SELFIES

AUGUST 01, 2015

TO BOOSE: I DREAMED ABOUT YOU, AGAIN.

I DREAMED WE WERE BACK IN HIGH SCHOOL AND GOING INTO CHEMISTRY class. It was where Mr. Brock's room was, but Mr. Little was our teacher. I thought that no one would believe that I was actually at school, so we'd better take a selfie to post on Facebook.

BECAUSE, AS YOU'LL CLEARLY RECALL, INTERNET, IPHONES, FACEBOOK, daily selfies . . . those were all a thing back in the day!

ANYWAY, CLASS HAD ALREADY STARTED, BUT I WAS UNWAVERING IN MY determination to push forward with that selfie. Well, I got a few. And just like today, they were all nose holes, half our heads, only one of us, or otherwise unflattering.

Never did either of us question why we looked like forty-year-old women! I woke up before we agreed on a photo to post.

40

ME, LORETTI, AND THEM PEANUT BUTTER CRACKERS

SEPTEMBER 04, 2016

I DREAMED THAT LORETTA LYNN MADE ME PEANUT BUTTER CRACKERS. I was *so* excited.

I woke up before I ate them, but I know they would've been the best ones ever.

41

ME & BOBBIE MCGEE

SEPTEMBER 20, 2016

I DREAMED I WENT TO A RECORD SHOP AND BOUGHT A JANIS JOPLIN CD. I reckon that's a good goal for the day.

42

ME, KENNY ROGERS & ALL THOSE NEIGHBOR BABIES

JANUARY 19, 2017

CHILDREN, I AM ABSOLUTELY EXHAUSTED. I TOOK CARE OF BABIES ALL night long! In my dream, that is. I dreamed that I offered to help my mom's neighbors with their kids.

What I didn't know is that they had two sets of triplets, two sets of twins, plus another child.

I ROUNDED UP ALL THE HELP I COULD FIND WHICH INCLUDED SOME Muncy Creek guys from high school, a couple going on their first date, some people from a cruise ship, and Kenny Rogers.

I kept losing the children in this museum the neighbors lived in. I mean, it was huge like a parking garage.

The children kept falling, peeing their pants, and just screwing with me in general because there were so dang many of them, I never could tell who I had fed and who I hadn't.

When the dream ended, all the children were in two locations. The boys were in the bathroom singing a *very* inappropriate Jimmy Buffett song, and the girls were trying to sneak off to go shopping.

I finally caught sight of the parents. The mom told me she was pregnant again, and I began to cry.

I don't know what this dream means, but for the love of God, please don't ask me to babysit.

43

LUCILLE GREEN & THE BEST CANDY IN THE WORLD

MARCH 03, 2017

TO LUCILLE GREEN: I DREAMED THAT YOU MADE ME A BOX FULL OF candy. I guess I ate every last drop because my thank you note said that I was bringing a needle, thread, and a sheet to you to sew me some clothes because nothing else fit.

44

ROBOT BUTLER

May 26, 2017

Not exactly a dream, but something that made me laugh. When I was a kid, I wanted a robot so it would bring me snacks.

As an adult, I still have that same dream.

Goals.

45

ME, DR. OZ & THE LIPSTICK

JUNE 25, 2017

I DREAMED I WENT BACK TO COLLEGE. DR. OZ WAS MY INSTRUCTOR.

I stopped by the bathroom before class. He was in there with his girlfriend. They were both putting on lipstick. It was Mary Kay. I liked the shade but was too intimidated to ask what the color was.

Then we were in the lecture hall. After he finished teaching, he asked if anyone had questions. I sure did.

Would you like to know what my question was? I was still hung up on that lipstick shade.

I raised my hand. He knew what I was gonna ask and chose someone else. I stood up and raised my hand. He chose someone else. I jumped up and down and raised my hand.

THERE WAS A SPOTLIGHT SHINING ON ME.

. . .

He. Chose. Someone. Else.

Why you gotta diss me like that, Dr. Oz? What kind of world do we live in when you can't even ask a man what shade of lipstick he's wearing!

46

BECKY HERON & MY COSTCO QUESTION

September 14, 2017

To Becky Heron: I dreamed about you last night.

I first dreamed that my cousin and I were stealing a kitten.

Why, I'm not sure. But I guess it could be said that we were literal cat burglars.

The dream then morphed to us being in a baby Costco. I was buying teeth whitener. The kit had four electric toothbrushes and a tube of itty bitty whitening toothpaste. It was $103. I keep saying that I needed to ask my dentist if it was ok to buy tooth whitener.

You were in the next aisle, so I hollered over and asked you. You said that since Kim and I were experienced at coloring our own hair at home, my cousin and I should be ok to whiten our teeth at home!

. . .

OK? IT WAS A PERFECTLY ACCEPTABLE ANSWER IN THE DREAM.

47

BOOSE, ME & THE EPIC FISH STORY

NOVEMBER 10, 2017

TO BOOSE: I DREAMED BRU, TYLER, AND I WERE FISHING. IT WAS awesome because I was catching these *huge* fish. Pretty sure we were on Cutshin.

We called it quits, and I told you how good the fishing was. You wanted to go, too. So, we headed toward the water.

We were going to the ocean.

BECAUSE MY DREAMS ARE SCREWY, AND THE OCEAN AND CUTSHIN GO hand in hand.

WE TOOK A SHORTCUT *THROUGH* OLIVE GARDEN—WHICH SOUNDS JUST like us. A customer asked where we were going. When we said we were going fishing, he said we'd never make it before dark.

I said, "You're probably right. Save us a breadstick."

. . .

WHICH SOUNDS JUST LIKE ME!

ANYWHO, WE EXITED THIS TWO STORY OLIVE GARDEN—WHICH WAS actually our old high school—and ran down the road to the Nixon Center. Which, again, is soooo close to the ocean!

WE SAW UNCLE POWERS AND STOPPED TO SAY HI. WE COULD SEE THIS very shallow ocean off in the distance, and we were trying so hard to get there.

The setting sun had given way to nighttime when I woke up. And it's too bad, too. I know we would have had an epic fish story to tell.

HEY, GETTING THERE IS HALF THE FUN. RIGHT?

SO, THE MORAL AND MESSAGE THIS DREAM WAS SENDING ME—CLEARLY—is that we need to go to Olive Garden.

48

THE TURNER HOUSE ON HURTS CREEK

May 07, 2018

Last night, I dreamed about the old Turner place on Hurts Creek.

I dreamed I drove by and saw lights on over there. So, I changed my plans and drove right up to the house.

For those of you unfamiliar with the Turner place, it's a white two story country home with a wraparound porch.

A true wraparound porch.

The home is nestled at the end of the road, backing up to the mountains. It's been vacant for many years.

Back to the dream . . .

. . .

As I pulled up to the house, I saw soft light spilling from the windows. A bunch of men were sitting on the right side of the porch. They were all dressed in dress pants, button down shirts, and hats—as if they were from a different era. I pulled away because I knew they didn't know me.

I drove for only a second before I turned back around. I didn't care that they didn't know me. They were about to.

I truly have always wanted to sit on that porch, so it's no surprise I'd dream about it.

49

TRACEY TURNER, THE BANANA SOURDOUGH BREAD & MY BLIND HUSBAND

June 29, 2018

To Tracey Turner: So, we were hanging out in my dream last night.

I dreamed you invited me and Bru for "dinner" at nine o'clock. Now, I *never* use the word dinner because it confuses me. Some people mean it as lunch. Some mean it for supper. I had no idea how you meant it, so I was panicking.

All of a sudden, Bru couldn't see, so we went to your and Ronnie's business because you were eye doctors.

You were examining him, and I walked up and whispered in his ear, "Ask her what she means about dinner!"

I mean, my husband was blind and all, but I had my priorities.

. . .

YOU FLAT OUT STATED THAT YOU MEANT SUPPER! AND YOU KNEW SOME people were hateful first thing in the morning because when you and Ronnie used to fly home for a visit, and you'd go to Mr. Hightower's class, it took him half the day to get turned around.

AGAIN, UM WHAT?

WE ALL KNOW MR. HIGHTOWER WAS THE JOLLIEST SOUL IN THAT school!

ANYWAY, MY NEAR BLIND HUSBAND DROVE US TO YOUR HOUSE IN THE country. You had baked fresh sourdough bread. You had it wrapped in a towel. I peeled the layers back, and it was perfect. Golden brown. It looked more like banana bread, but you said it was sourdough, so daggone it, it was sourdough.

ANYWAY, ALL OF A SUDDEN, THE BREAD WAS MYSTERIOUSLY SLICED—I'M guessing we had my blind husband do it.

We all—you, me, and Kam—picked up our bread, made toasts like wine, and I was just about to take a bite when I woke up!

NOW I'M STARVING, WANT BANANA SOURDOUGH BREAD, AND WONDER IF you'd share your recipe?

50

THE CRAZED CHICKEN MAN

I POSTED THIS TO FACEBOOK, thinking it was a dream. Turns out, lots of Leslie County people remember this fella. Everyone's account is a little different, but still, I thought I'd include it in my crazy dream journal:

JULY 10, 2018

THIS IS GONNA SOUND STRANGE. LC FOLKS, I NEED YOU TO TRAVEL back in time with me to the 1970s. I think it was the week leading up to the festival. The booths were set up on the playground at Hyden Elementary. The booth in question was at or near the dugout just below the funeral home.

THINK THIRD BASE.

I HAVE A MEMORY, A RATHER VIVID ONE, OF A CAGED MAN. HE WAS

crazed and taunting the crowd. He was all over the place—more like a gorilla than a man. Sometimes he was curled up in the corner, other times he was lurching at the onlookers, clawing at a chain link fence, and spewing incoherent words.

His mere presence scared the life out of me. What he did next *scarred* the life out of me. There was a chicken in the cage with him. In a psychotic rage, he grabbed it and bit its head off.

Is that even possible?

I've always had bizarre dreams. So, this could simply be a crazy dream from my childhood. If so, some diagnostic testing was probably missed somewhere along the way!

51

THE UN-DEAD LADY

July 21, 2018

I dreamed we were at the "funeral" of a woman who wasn't dead.

She was sure it would happen, so she called us all together. She was a robust elderly lady who was spry as could be, and who had a sharp wit.

She wore a floral dress and pearls. She was the lady from the British show, Keeping Up Appearances.

She announced that her time was upon her, bid us adieu, and climbed into the coffin, partially closing the lid.

She'd give the side eye every now and then, play peek-a-boo, and even would rise to perform a comedy act from time to time.

. . .

FINALLY, SHE DECIDED THAT IT WASN'T HER TIME, SO SHE CLIMBED OUT and offered her funeral to someone else.

I THINK I'VE JUST SEEN MY FUNERAL.

52

KNOCKING BACK BOURBON

August 02, 2018

I dreamed last night that Bru and I were throwing back bourbon. We were having a good old time.

I woke up with a headache.

I'm the only person I know who lives it up in my dream and who wakes up paying the consequences.

53

AND YOU WERE THERE. AND YOU . . .

SEPTEMBER 17, 2018

CHILDREN, I AM WORE SMACK-DAB OUT! YOU KNOW HOW IN THE Wizard of Oz, after Dorothy takes her fall, and she's telling everyone that they were in her dream?

"AND YOU WERE THERE, AND YOU WERE THERE. AND YOU . . ."

WELL, I HAD A DREAM LIKE THAT WITH ALL OF LESLIE COUNTY AND half of Richmond.

I DREAMED THAT BOOSE, KIM, AND I WERE CHILDREN. MOM HAD TAKEN us to her friend, Kathy's, house to play. It was Michelle Moore and Jennifer Asher's old house on Rockhouse. At some point, we were in this house. Then, the dream would morph to us being in an old house on Hurts Creek.

. . .

AT ONE POINT, ALL US KIDS ENDED UP IN A VACANT, HAUNTED HOUSE. We didn't see any ghosts, but we were so wild, we could've run out demons! This house bore a striking resemblance to Hyden Elementary. We were racing on the steps. When it was my turn to race, I looked over to see who I was up against. The kid was Tyler. My kid. But, we were the same age.

Neither of us thought this was off.

AFTER ALL THAT, I GOT SICK AND HAD TO SEE THE SCHOOL NURSE, TARA Mann Alcorn. I was positive I had the flu. Lucky for me, the nurse was available at that vacant, haunted elementary school house. She shoved a nine foot thermometer in my mouth—the kind you'd use in chemistry class. I watched that giant red mercury line racing toward the end. I asked her if there was one line or two. She assured me it wasn't *that* sort of test, told me I didn't have the flu, and basically said, "Suck it up!" I love you, girl, but you really have no bedside manner.

ANYWAY, WE MORPHED BACK TO THE MOORE HOUSE ON ROCKHOUSE. BY this time, someone had entered us in a competition—probably our parents who we hadn't laid eyes on in this dream town! Tim Morgan made the mistake of showing Boose and me how to drive a forklift. So, while our teammates were slaving trying to win this Breakout style competition, we we're outside moving rock piles and having a *big* old time.

ONCE WE WERE DONE, BOOSE AND I MOVED BACK INSIDE WHERE WE decided to jump on the beds for a while. The beds were about fifteen feet up in the air, so we had to work hard to get on them. Too bad those forklifts weren't available.

. . .

So, once we did all that, we had to submit a typed report for the judging. We rushed our paperwork to Kayla Powell because absolutely no one could type faster than her. *But,* on the way to Kayla, we had to take the little red wagon to David Maggard Jr and his friend. And, in doing so, we had to pull each other around the house some first.

Shew.

So, if any of y'all were ever thinking that Boose and I would make good teammates, this goes to prove that, while you'd dang sure have fun, we might not be your first choice if winning is the end goal!

54

I'M GOING, TOO!

SEPTEMBER 26, 2018

I DREAMED THAT BRU LEFT ME. I WAS SO MAD THAT I PACKED MY BAGS and went with him.

I DON'T THINK I FULLY GRASPED THAT *LEAVING* BUSINESS.

55

EUGENIA, RONNIE CAROL, PEGGY LYNN, SHARON HUFF, ME, BOOSE, HUNGRY EYES & HANGRY BELLIES

October 17, 2018

To Eugenia Napier: The other night, I had a dream about you.

I dreamed that you, me, Mom, Ronnie Carol Stewart, Sharon Huff, and Boose were all sitting on a roof watching a new house being roofed across the road.

No sneaky nosey neighbors in this bunch. We were right up there showing them exactly what we were about!

Anyway, at some point, we all started singing Hungry Eyes. It went from that to talking about cheesecake.

As the dream ended, you were backing down a ladder to go get us all cheesecake. Meanwhile, the rest of us were still up on this roof singing Hungry Eyes.

I DON'T KNOW IF YOU WERE GETTING FIRST DIBS ON THAT CHEESECAKE or getting away from our singing!

56

OUT LIE THAT PREACHER & BAD FIRST DATE

October 20, 2018

Children, I am *tard* today!

I made dressing *all* night in my sleep *and* helped two people move.

TWO.

We tried donating stuff to an organization on Preacher's Fork, and I had to out *lie* a *preacher* to get them to take my stuff!

I SUCCEEDED.

. . .

I WRANGLED DOGS ON HURRICANE CREEK, AND I CHECKED MAIL FROM three mailboxes seventy-five feet up in the air.

I went to school and had a first date with someone who didn't want to go.

I WISH MY DREAM PEOPLE WOULD SETTLE THE HECK DOWN BECAUSE THEY are wearing me out. Shew.

IF ANYBODY NEEDS ME TODAY, I WILL PUNCH YOU RIGHT IN THE THROAT for even considering asking!

57

AMY, THE CHICKEN FARMER

October 28, 2018

Last night, I dreamed that I was gonna try my hand at farming. I started by buying a bazillion chicken eggs that would hatch under any care whatsoever.

Since they were sprawled across the field like pumpkins in a pumpkin patch, I decided I needed a place for my future fluffy chickens to roost and lay eggs. All of a sudden, I bewitched a black barn, complete with egg collection shoots, into existence on my barren mud field.

Then, it was time to get down to "farming."

I started cracking my eggs, which looked exactly as you'd imagine a sunny side up, uncooked egg to look. When I'd cracked about a dozen into my bowl, I had the horrific thought that I don't like to get up early, so I quit cracking "birthing" those baby chickens.

. . .

I WOKE UP TO A FEW PROFOUND THOUGHTS:

(1) Which came first on my farm, the chicken or the egg? The egg.

(2) I obviously didn't understand how egg hatching worked since I was helping.

(3) Not sure I even remotely understand the concept of farming.

(4) I was about to have some real bad mornings of getting up early when those other eggs hatched on their own!

(5) I'm a bad chicken mom.

(6) I kinda want an omelet.

58

MARILYN LOVETT & THE SCUBA DIVER

October 30, 2018

To Mom: I dreamed last night that cousin Marilyn was Mammaw and Pappaw's caregiver.

I went to Aunt Pat's trailer and in walked Marilyn. I asked why she wasn't with Mammaw and Pappaw on vacation. She said it was her days off, and the last she heard, Mammaw was scuba diving!

We should probably fire her.

59

#1 BULLDOG FAN

November 09, 2018

I dreamed we had moved to Florida. It was a nightmare! I was upset because I was gonna have to be a Bulldog fan.

Ok?

I can promise you that in my waking world, the words "Florida Bulldogs" have never once crossed my mind!

I was also upset because it's hot there, and my hair would be flat. As I woke up, I was on the bus with an elderly gang of mean old women. The ring leader had her recliner on the bus. She meant business. I've never been so happy to wake up early in all my life. Shew!

60

TINA TURNER & THE POWDERED SUGAR

November 15, 2018

Last night, I dreamt I was cleaning off a stage for Tina Turner. She was making her way toward the stage on a walkway through the audience. She was singing and dancing and making her signature "stank face."

I was up on this stage on my hands and knees swiping frantically at the stage floor. It was covered in powdered sugar. I have no idea why, or why I was the one having to clean it, but Tina was sashaying toward the stage a lot faster than I was cleaning.

She saw I was trying to get it ready. She nodded at me and smiled and continued to perform.

The dream shifted before she got to the stage. By this time, I was standing on the walkway where Tina had been performing. All of a sudden, the microphone was thrust into my hands, and I was voluntold to announce some children as they descended the steps as they were leaving the school.

The first little girl walked down the steps. I glanced at her and went straight into a spiel about her hair being crocheted. It was exactly like a Cabbage Patch doll's hair. I was just starting into a weird number about the other girl's strange hair when the dream shifted again.

This time, it was a darker dream full of danger and fear.

I'M SUDDENLY STARTING TO THINK THAT WASN'T POWDERED SUGAR ON that stage . . .

61

DREAMWEAVER

November 22, 2018—my birthday

Last night, I dreamed about my cousin, Dee Dee. I dreamed we were teenagers again. There was a boy I liked who didn't like me. She told me I was trying too hard and to just be myself.

So, I went and took a shower, wrapped up in a towel, and walked into the common room where he and a whole slew of people were. I walked over to this curved couch, plopped down, stretched out, and went to sleep.

Somehow, I don't think that's exactly what she meant.

62

FANCY

December 03, 2018

I dreamed I was on a date with Jason Momoa. We both wore footed pajamas.

I'm bound to be fancy yet!

63

THREE NIGHTMARES & THE SECRET ROOM

For this entry, I don't have specific dates because these dreams occurred over a span of thirty years.

None of the dreams are related, but for reasons I don't fully understand, these recurring dreams resolved themselves due to a scenario that happened in the final dream.

One of the dreams, I fully understand why it occurred and why it stopped. The other three, even though I grasp the reasoning they stopped, I don't understand the purpose they held in my life.

The Doorbell

Growing up, in our house on Hurricane, we had two front doors. The primary one we used was upstairs, but both doors were functional and had doorbells. And each doorbell had a distinct chime.

. . .

I USED TO HAVE A RECURRING NIGHTMARE THAT ONE DOORBELL WOULD chime. I'd go to the appropriate door, open it to find no one there, only to hear the chime for the other door.

I'd change course and head to the other door only to hear the tone for the previous one. This would continue until I would wake from my dream, heart pounding and terrified.

IN THEORY, THIS SHOULDN'T HAVE BEEN A SCARY DREAM SINCE NOTHING actually happened. Somehow, though, in the dream, I knew someone was toying with me. His intentions were cruel.

I always woke up panic-stricken and thankful to have been pulled from my nightmare.

THIS DREAM CONTINUED FOR YEARS.

THE FINAL TIME I DREAMED IT, THE SEQUENCE OF DOORBELL TAG continued as usual.

When the last doorbell sounded, I opened it as I always had. But this time, when no one was there, I went in search of him.

His car was parked in the driveway, and there he sat on the hood. He was smiling and laughing at our game.

I wasn't scared, and I wasn't even angry at what he'd put me through. This man was someone I knew—for real. He was neither a friend nor a foe, so why my final dream revealed him to be the person who had tormented me, I will never know.

BUT, FACING MY FEARS STOPPED THIS DREAM. I WAS ABOUT TWENTY years old the last time I had the dream. That was twenty-seven years ago, so it's been a minute.

As long as this retelling doesn't summon it back up, I think I can close the proverbial chapter on that particular nightmare.

The Tidal Wave

I used to have a recurring nightmare that I was at the beach. I would walk out on a pier. The day was peaceful, and the pier was vacant.

As I moved closer to the end, I'd see a wave building rapidly. The sea would rise, becoming level with the end of the pier. Then the tidal wave would form.

I'd turn to run, only to find that the path I had previously taken was now boarded up.

I was trapped.

I'd turn to look back. The wave was close enough to touch. Just before it crashed into me, I'd wake up—trembling and on the verge of tears.

I know why I dreamed this. If you've ever found yourself in an impossible situation, you can probably relate to these feelings of entrapment.

Once that situation was remedied, I never had the dream again.

The House at the Edge of the Garden

If we've been friends for a minute, you likely know that I find familiarity in eras that I have never visited and with generations far beyond my years.

If it wasn't for my love of all things eighties, I'd swear I was born in the wrong generation.

I have an old soul that took a while to catch up with me. And the older I get, the older it gets—if that makes sense.

Back to the journal . . .

I have a recurring dream. It's a nightmare, but I can't say specifically why.

In the dream, there's a house. This house sits in the edge of Uncle Fred's garden across from where my house sat on Hurricane. Only, this dream house doesn't exist. And as far as I know, it never did.

This house is at the edge of the creek, the back of the home backing up to the water. It faces Preacher's Fork. It's a two-story, wood panel framed house painted in white. The roof is sloped, its tin construction tinged in streaks of rust. It's old. It's dingy. And it's spooky.

The house is haunted—two entities watch me from the upstairs window. They're always there.

Time after time, I dreamt of this house. And time after time, I'd wake up frightened, the feeling of dark energy all around me.

It was the kind of dream that you couldn't shake off fast enough.

The last time I dreamt of this house, all the physicality's of the home were the same—the location, the construction, the apparitions watching through a veiled curtain from the upstairs window . . .

The negative energy surrounding this house made me physically ill.

Still yet, I walk closer, my eyes trained on the upstairs window.

THEY'RE THERE, WATCHING ME.

I MOVE ACROSS THE PROPERTY, ONTO THE PORCH, AND WALK CLOSER TO the white door. It has three horizontal panels at the bottom and a widow in the top half of the door. Another curtain prevents me from seeing inside.

The doorknob is antique, an oil-rubbed bronze that's weathered from age. I turn the knob and walk inside.

I don't remember any of the downstairs of the house, but suddenly I'm upstairs in the bedroom they constantly occupy.

I'M SCARED. BUT THERE'S NO TURNING BACK NOW.

I SWEEP MY EYES FROM SIDE TO SIDE, FRANTICALLY LOOKING FOR THEM. My heart pounds in my chest. They're not there. Suddenly, I'm not scared anymore, those feelings of fear quickly falling away.

THE ROOM IS FULLY FURNISHED, OUTFITTED WITH DECOR FROM centuries past. There's two full beds in the room with homemade quilts topping each. There's a spinning wheel near the window. I move closer to investigate.

Suddenly, I find myself peering out the window through veiled curtains.

. . .

As I awoke from that dream, I did so without feelings of trepidation and without the aura of dark energy—or any energy at all.

Again, facing my fears caused this dream to disappear from my nighttime escapades.

As for the two people in the window, I've often wondered if they both represented me—the me who was afraid and the me who faced my fears.

I'm no doctor, and I'm not too hung up on dreams having profound meaning. Although, these nightmares had a profound enough impact that I gave them their own chapter, so what do I know?

All I know for certain is that it's been years since I dreamed any of them. I pray that trend continues.

Now for the final recurring dream in this chapter, the one that actually wasn't a nightmare.

Allow me to give a little backstory for this one . . .

I grew up on Hurricane Creek, a holler in Southeastern Kentucky. It was the best place on earth to be a kid. I have countless wonderful memories there.

However, when I was nineteen, our house burned, and we lost everything we had.

I dream of the house from time to time, less as the years have passed.

THIS DREAM IS ABOUT THE HOUSE AND A ROOM THAT NEVER EXISTED.

THE SECRET ROOM

I USED TO HAVE A RECURRING DREAM ABOUT OUR HOUSE THAT BURNED. I would dream that I'd go back and everything was exactly as it always was. I'd question why I hadn't gone back home before then.

OTHER TIMES, I'D DREAM THAT I'D WALK IN AND SMELL SMOKE OR SEE charred boards.

Another variation is that we'd come into money and rebuilt our home as an exact replica of the one I recalled.

SOMETIMES, STILL, I DREAM THAT I'VE GONE HOME. IT FEELS LIKE HOME, but looks nothing like the one we knew. That realization only occurs upon waking up. In the dream, nothing is amiss.

THEN THERE'S THE DREAM, THE ONE I'VE WORKED ALL NIGHT TO TELL, where I walk into the living room only to discover something new in our old house.

IN OUR HOME, WE HAD A BIG BAY WINDOW IN THE LIVING ROOM. IT HAD, probably, twelve panes of glass and bowed out into a semicircle beyond the outer walls.

In my memory, it covered the majority of the front wall of the living room. But in my dream, another room sat just to the left of the window.

Time after time, I'd dream that I went home and was looking around the living room. I'd spot a room that piqued my interest greatly. I'd walk toward the room but wake up every time before I walked inside.

This dream occurred for years.

FINALLY, THE LAST NIGHT I DREAMED ABOUT THE SECRET ROOM, I walked into the living room and spotted this room that I'd never seen.

I moved closer.

Always before, I woke up just before I walked through the entryway.

NOT THIS TIME.

THE ROOM WAS DIMLY LIT AND WINDOWLESS. IT WAS A SMALL CUTOUT that bumped out even with the bay window.

A curved bar with two bar stools occupied the space, the odd amenities situated in the center of the room. The bar top had a brown leather edge that was raised, the padded rim bordering the half-circle.

The only other thing to occupy the space was sheet music. It was strewn all about the bar, the bar stools, and haphazardly all across the floor in every direction.

It was as if someone had held a stack of sheet music high in the air and just let it go a few sheets at a time. The pages would have scattered out, fanning onto and beyond the bar.

SINCE THE DAY I DREAMT OF FINALLY EXPLORING THE SECRET ROOM, I'VE never dreamt of it since.

. . .

If I put stock into dreams, I'd say that perseverance is key to peace—the "what ifs" in life can be as detrimental as anything. And you can quote me on that one.

I now return you to your regularly scheduled program—My Crazy Dreams . . .

64

REPUBLICAN BUTTERFLIES OR LIBERAL BUTTERFLIES

JANUARY 08, 2019

MOM, LAST NIGHT I DREAMED THAT YOU, ME, CLAY, AND SOME MAN were in a room. You we're talking about butterflies.

NOT THE FLYING SORT.

YOU SAID THAT WHEN REPUBLICANS GET BUTTERFLIES, THEY GET THEM in their butt. When liberals get butterflies, they get them in their thighs.

Clay was swinging on a porch swing in this room. He said, "I get them in my butt!" He just kept right on swinging.

THE GUY GOT OFFENDED, STATED THAT HE GOT BUTTERFLIES IN HIS thighs, and stormed out!

. . .

So, If you learn nothing from this dream, take this advice—you can't talk about people's butts and thighs. Ok? They get testy.

65

OF ALL THE DREAMS I'VE EVER HAD, THIS IS MY VERY FAVORITE. IT'S NOT MY USUAL CRAZY DREAM. THIS ONE HAD SUCH DEEP MEANING. I CALL IT THE CANE POLE.

February 20, 2019

I just woke up from a terribly sweet dream. I'm not sure how it was possible, but somehow, inexplicably, I met my grandfather from many generations ago.

This was my Pappaw Lovett's many times removed great grandfather.

In my dream, generation after generation spilled into this little white single-story house. There stood our grandfather, so happy to meet us all. He wore bib overalls and a white shirt underneath. His skin was dark complected and leathery. Weary, even. He'd lived a hard life.

. . .

At one point, we realized that he couldn't identity with our current generation, and we all went on our way.

We scattered far and wide and resumed our modern day living.

At some point, we all congregated once more in this little house. That's when we realized that, while we had gone about our way to continue with our modern conveniences, our grandfather had not.

He couldn't relate to us. That much was true. But he hadn't given up on us. When we piled back into this room in droves, we saw that he had been working the whole time while we were off enjoying the gadgets of each of our eras.

His back was turned to us while he continued his work. Cane poles of varying sizes filled this room. It was a spectacular sight. They ranged in size from two feet to seven. The knobby poles with strings hanging from the end of each was the perfect size for each one of his descendants.

He told us that, while our worlds were very different from his in so many ways, he wanted to provide us with a skill that we all would benefit from. He wanted to teach us to fish.

It was a sweet dream with a powerful message. Sometimes people give you the best they can from where they are in life. And even if that looks different than the best you have to offer, it doesn't put any less value on it.

66

THAT TIME I WAS QUEEN OF ENGLAND

February 21, 2019

I dreamed that my friend, who I've never seen before in my life, was the Queen of England. We were talking, and I casually mentioned that it was so weird that we were *both* the Queen of England.

She was surprised that I had been and asked when that was. I searched my memory and sure couldn't recall. So, I turn to Bru to help me fill in the blanks.

"Bru, when was I the Queen of England?"

He gives me that "Bru look" that I've seen twenty gazillion times! He informs me that I was *never* the Queen of England.

It was embarrassing that he couldn't remember because that shore as shiz happened!

. . .

ANYWAY, I TURN TO MY FRIEND AND TELL HER THAT I CAN'T RECALL THE dates, but every time I threw a party, we listened to nothing but Queen . . . which sounds like a royal decree I would put in place.

AS THE DREAM ENDED, I GOT THE CURRENT QUEEN IN ALL KINDS OF trouble with her people because we threw an unruly party and allowed the press in.

We were giving drunken interviews as I woke up. It was hysterical.

67

ANGIE LUCAS, AMANDA MASSEY, ME & SIR ELTON JOHN SNOOTYPANTS

February 28, 2019

Last night, I dreamed about Sir Elton John.

I dreamed that my friends, Angie Lucas and Amanda Massey bought this huge piece of property deep in a holler and invited us all over for a cookout. All the neighbors came, including Elton John.

We were all gathered 'round, including Elton, and we were all talking, and talking, and talking.

Sooooo, I look at my new friends and strike up a conversation of my own. I ask, "So, are y'all from 'round here?"

One of these things is not like the other . . .

. . .

Elton looks baffled as can be. He says, "I'm British. Can't you tell by my accent?"

I said, "Well, I just thought you had a British nanny who talked to you non-stop, and that's why you sounded that way."

He couldn't believe his ears. So I, speaking in my best British accent, tried to mimic what their conversations would sound like. I said, "Elton, are you ready for your soup beans and taters?"

I'm pretty sure I was on to something. But, Sir Elton Snootypants would not go along with my theory.

68

GIRLTIME & GRUB FUND

March 18, 2019

Last night, I dreamed that my cousin, Boose, and I started a Go-Fund-Me for lunch. In it, we stated clearly that we had money, but we wanted someone else to pay for Girltime & Grub.

(That's really what we call it when we get together.)

You all came through for us. When I woke up, we'd acquired forty-five dollars!

In the dream, our very first donation came from the mayor of our hometown.

She loves us in real life, and we love her, so I wouldn't have expected anything less!

69

WE SOME BAD CHAMPIONS, MY FRIEND

MARCH 20, 2019

I DREAMED MOM AND I WERE AT A SCHOOL TALENT SHOW AT THE OLD Hyden Elementary Gym. The whole school had congregated in the gym. We were thoroughly enjoying the show when this boy and girl got up to sing We Are The Champions.

THEY WERE DOING GREAT UNTIL THE KEYBOARDIST KEPT INTERJECTING random notes.

I LEANED OVER TO MOM AND WHISPERED, "THEIR KEYBOARD PLAYER IS awful!"

SHE LOOKED HORRIFIED AND LOOKED DOWN.

. . .

TURNS OUT, *I* WAS THE ACCIDENTAL KEYBOARD PLAYER. I HAD A GUITAR in my lap. It had keys on it like a piano, but it was clearly a guitar.

MADE BY PLAYSKOOL, I IMAGINE!

ANYWAY, EVERY TIME I RESTED MY ELBOWS ON MY LAP, I WAS PLAYING A little tune for them.

TURNS OUT, WE SURELY WERE *NOT* THE CHAMPIONS, MY FRIEND.

70

HURRICANE CREEK REUNION & HANK WILLIAMS, JR.

March 29, 2019

Hurricane Creekers, we were hanging out in my dreams last night. More specifically, we were all congregating on Burton Hill. Neighbors came from far and wide to join us.

In some parts of the dream, we reminisced about the old cabin that used to sit above the rock in the curve. In other parts of the dream, we had all come together to rebuild a replica.

Some speculated that it used to be an old mill.

As neighbors congregated, we all sat on the porch of the cabin and devised a plan to gather old family recipes and come up with a Hurricane Creek Cookbook.

. . .

Farris Burton and James were still with us in the dream, along with Ruth and Vance Bowling. Hank Williams, Jr was also there.

Um, Ok?

Ruth's signature garden wasn't down by the creek, but all the children were down there splashing around.

It was a truly wonderful dream with lots of familiar faces.

71

CHERYL PARDINGTON, MAMMAW, ME, AND MAYHAM

April 13, 2019

To my friend, Cheryl Pardington: I dreamed about you, and it was awful.

I dreamed you came to visit. So, I thought I'd take you sightseeing. For some reason, we had to drive separately, and the very first place I took you to was the roughest house in the county.

This place doesn't exist in real life.

Anyway, you and my little Mammaw went on ahead of me. When I got there, I was mortified that I'd sent you there. It was a mess with dangerous people everywhere. The owners weren't home. You and Mammaw had done a little cooking before I got there. She was packing around a glass bottle of fresh milk. So, I'm guessing you milked some cows before I got there, too!

WHEN I GOT TO THE HOUSE, I DROVE RIGHT UP TO IT. PRETTY standard.

SO, THE TIME CAME FOR ME TO LEAVE, AND I WAS WALKING TOWARD THE door. I encountered a fella who played some sort of shiny brass instrument—a trumpet, I think. Anyway, every time I'd say something to him, he'd respond in trumpet. And, apparently I was fluent because I understood every word.

SOOO, IT WAS FINALLY TIME FOR ME TO WALK TO MY CAR. YOU AND Mammaw had left before me, trumpet guy slowing me down. When I walked out on the porch, the car I parked in the driveway wasn't there. What *was* there was an obstacle course, like American Ninja Warrior. Honest to God, it was like Hotel California in a Kentucky holler! "You can check in anytime you like, but you can never leave!"

SO I'M GOING ALONG THIS OBSTACLE COURSE—WHICH DANGLED OVER A cliff. There were these big knobby knobs that you had to grasp, then you'd alternate hands to swing yourself along this stretch of obstacle course. All I kept thinking as I progressed through this playground of horrors was that Mammaw did this one handed because she had that bottle of milk!

ANYWAY, *IF* YOU MADE IT, A BUS WAS WAITING TO TAKE YOU TO YOUR car. There wasn't many people on the bus. And, I suspect if that bus had had a vanity plate, it would've been called, "The Struggle Bus!"

. . .

So, I finally make it to you all. I apologize for taking you on such a journey. You looked at me and said, "I don't ever want to drive on those little windy roads. EVER AGAIN!" You didn't say anything about the little house of horrors or the obstacle course!

When I woke up, we were on our way to the Big House.

Not *that* Big House!

I knew the beauty of that mountainside cabin in my little hometown would make up for all you'd gone through.

72

MARLENE SHEALEY, FREDDY KRUEGER, ME & THAT SOUTHEASTERN KENTUCKY ACCENT

May 07, 2019

Last night, I dreamed I was on a movie set. A horror movie. In the dream, my cousin, Marlene, was going to be starring in the latest Nightmare on Elm Street movie. *Sooo,* the whole family came to watch her acting debut.

Only, when we got there, Marlene was too afraid to keep the role.

You can imagine where this is going . . .

So there I sit in the Star role!

. . .

For some reason, everyone who was supposed to be in this movie had bailed. All of them. All my family who had gone to see Marlene's movie debut was now in this movie.

All of us were from Eastern Kentucky.

The movie set was a charming vintage dining room with fabric wallpaper, big chunky antique furniture, and an oval dining room table that had a long tablecloth that skirted the floor on all sides. Six of us were seated at the table. Plates were positioned in front of us with bowls of yummy looking cream colored chowder in the center of each.

I don't recall the director calling, "Action," but somehow, we knew to begin . . .

Oh, did I fail to mention that this movie was set in England?

Sooo, in walks Freddie Krueger. He stands at the head of the table wearing his signature red and green striped shirt and dark pants. He fans his razor fingers out, pulsing them. An ominous smile crosses his face.

He speaks in his frightening tone. "And, what are we doing?"

The question is directed at me. I freeze. In all the excitement, I realize that I forgot to learn Marlene's lines.

. . .

Freddie clanks his razor fingers together and repeats the question.

I reply in my Kentucky twang that was suppose to be an English accent, "I'm just sitting here eating this chowder."

Then my castmates follow suit, talking about their soup . . .

The director throws his papers in the air and yells, "CUT! Don't say a word. None of you. Not. One. Word!"

Freddie got a kick out of it, but I'm pretty sure that ended our acting careers. I'm also fairly certain that "fifteen minutes" of fame was more like five seconds.

Anyway, I know I'm an actress now, but I promise not to let it change me.

73

POUR SOME AQUA NET ON ME

May 29, 2019

I dreamed that I was standing at this table with a bunch of other women who looked to be my age. They were strangers.

Someone was pouring pop into clear glasses. Maybe it was beer.

She was pouring it fast, so the carbonation was causing the liquid in the cup to rise up to twice its volume.

I pointed to a cup with an especially frothy top. I said, "I grew up in the Aqua Net generation. That was our hair!"

74

ANGIE LUCAS, AMY COLLINS, THE PUBLISHED BOOK & THE DECLARATION

June 10, 2019

Last night, my dream world was active!

I dreamed I was sitting at a table with Angie Lucas and Amy Collins. It was my high school Biology class. Angie was sitting in the middle with Amy to her right. Angie had written a book, and we were all looking at it. I have no idea what it was about, but I was moved to tears.

I turned to her and said, "You're a published author! You have no idea how much people love you!" She tried to push away those words with modesty. So, I pinned her with a teary stare and repeated those words. I said, "You truly don't realize how much people love you!" Then, I turned to Amy and said, "Both of you. They love you both."

. . .

AMY ALMOST LAUGHED AND REPLIED, "I'M AMY FREAKIN' COLLINS! I can have any man I'd like!"

ONE OF THESE THINGS WAS MORE HUMBLE THAN THE OTHER!

NOTE: AND IF YOU ARE FORTUNATE ENOUGH TO KNOW "AMY *FREAKIN'* Collins," you know that never in a million years would she say something like that! That's what made it so funny in the dream.

75

THAT TIME I FELL ON THE QUEEN OF ENGLAND

June 14, 2019

Lord, children, I've had me a traumatic night of dreams! I dreamed I fell on the Queen of England.

Just in case you wonder, her royal subjects didn't take kindly to that and became a royal pain in my bahookie!

It all started at a wedding in this huge cathedral. I was asked to come up and put some kind of rings on these big pipe organ pipes. A man wanted me to choose the yellow one. There was no yellow one, so I just placed the ring all Willy Nilly on the cream colored one. They were *all* cream colored, so I didn't think it would matter. Turns out, my role was to choose the wife of the groom.

Oops.

. . .

SOO, HE GETS ALL TORE UP BECAUSE I'VE CHOSEN THE WRONG WOMAN for him. Soo, I suggest that he mix some paint and make yellow, and we'll paint this organ pipe that I mistaking chose. Problem solved. He thinks that's a dandy idea, so we mix this magical paint that has just appeared beside me out of thin air. We pour it in the tube, and it bubbles up all around and cascades down the steps, as if we were pouring vinegar in a tube of baking soda.

IT MADE A HUGE MESS, BUT THE GUARDS WERE APPEASED AND FINALLY took their guns off me—they were bad tore up that I'd chosen the wrong woman for him *then* made a huge mess in the church!

I LOOK UP AND SEE A FELLA IN THE BALCONY SEATING WITH A RATHER curious tablet. It was space age looking with antennas and other doodads protruding from the four sides. I realize he's with the Queen, so I think he must have way better WiFi than the rest of us. So, I hop on up there to inquire.

IN THE PROCESS OF MY INQUISITION—WHICH HE WASN'T APPRECIATING— I lose my footing and fall on the Queen.

SHE WAS NONE TOO HAPPY THAT I WAS SPRAWLED OUT ON HER LIKE A swimmer belly surfing on a surfboard. We looked like a turtle. Her royal hooligans came after me once more . . .

THE SCENE CHANGES, AND I'M NOW SITTING IN A ROCKING CHAIR, ON A porch, on a hillside home in rural Appalachia. I see my family making their way up the dirt road in their beat up truck, and I stand to greet them. I'm an old woman now. When I stand up, I realize that the queen infected me with her royalness. I stand about nine feet tall, which astonishes my family and myself.

THEN, WHEN I SPEAK, I HAVE A BRITISH ACCENT. SCARED THE SHIITAKE out of me!

SO, THAT'S THE FULL STORY OF THAT TIME I FELL ON THE QUEEN OF England, became British, and nine feet tall!

76

OMG, IT'S ELTON JOHN

August 09, 2019

I dreamt I saw Elton John in the Dollar Tree at home. It was located a few doors down from the shoe store.

The clerk and I were having a random conversation about him when I turned around, and there he was.

He flashed a megawatt smile and was wearing his signature unique sunglasses.

Anyway, when I saw him, I screamed, "Oh my God! It's ELTON JOHN!"

I ran towards him, that megawatt smile quickly twisting into a look of horror!

. . .

I SNATCHED HIM TO ME AND GAVE HIM A HUGE HUG. HE SURELY DIDN'T want it, but he stood there and took it.

77

CAINT NOBODY TORNADO IN A DRESS

August 26, 2019

I dreamed that Johnny Paul called me and told me there was a tornado coming. I was trying to get Granny out of the trailer and up on the hill. She was completely wheelchair bound, and I *had* to get pants on her. Apparently, you can't tornado in a dress. You just *"caint."*

What's worse, I was having to drive the clunker. What's worse than that is that people had to move *their cars* so I could get up the hill. Then, I was worried I wouldn't be able to keep the car from rolling once I did get her up there!

But, before I accomplished any of that, the dream changed to me seeing a bunch of foreign guys across the county—Bob Fork area. I guess Granny was waiting for the tornado to come get her because JP and I were across the county shooting the shiz with the foreigners.

. . .

Then, they made him mad. So we had to kick their hindends. All of them. There were about six of them.

By the time we blinked back to Hurricane, the sun was shining, and Granny was bout to kill us both! She was sitting at the edge of the steps, in her wheelchair . . . still wearing her dress!

My dream people need to settle the heck down, and I need a nap!

78

WENDOVER & ITS NEIGHBORING COMMUNITY, CANADA

August 31, 2019

Last night, I dreamt that Camilla Parker Bowles—Prince Charles' wife—walked us all over Canada.

Canada was about three minutes from Wendover. When we got to the Fish and Game Club, I commented how I didn't realize how close Canada was to Wendover.

I assure you, had I *walked* that much, that would *not* have been my bloody comment.

I don't know why I dream about those royals so often. But they are a *royal* pain in my bahookie!

79

THE DRIVE-IN & THE LIE

October 16, 2019

To Cassie Green Bradley: I dreamed about you.

I dreamed that we were at this house where the old drive-in theatre was back home. There was a sheet on the floor with various vintage items scattered across it. Among them were two speakers that you'd hang on your window. They looked totally different.

You said, "Dad got these for me when they tore down the drive-in. I knew you'd want one."

I snatched one up and was so excited to get it! I said, "Thank you so much, Cassie! Which one were you wanting?"

. . .

You had a perplexed look on your face. You said, "I was wanting that one," and pointed to the one I was holding.

We started laughing. I said, "I picked it up to hand to you!" You knew I was lying, but it sounded exactly like something I'd do in real life.

80

WATCHING DREAMS THROUGH JOEL BRASHEAR'S VIDEOS

October 22, 2019

I had the best dream. It may seem like nothing special to most, but I visited with a lot of familiar faces in this dream.

In the dream, I watched the entire thing through videos that Joel Brashear had put together.

It started with people racing at the Big House. Of all the places they could have chosen to conduct this race on the grounds of Wendover, it was held in the living room—between the fireplace and the bookshelves. If you're not familiar with the Big House, that space is a total of about four steps.

One of the races included four people - - two people I didn't know, Mom, and Kim - pre broke foot. Mom smoked them every time! They ran several "laps." But Mom won every single time.

JOEL WAS INTERVIEWING A LADY WHO'D BEEN A CANADIAN TRACK STAR in her heyday. Kim, Mom, and the other two people were standing behind them in the background while they were conducting this interview. The lady pointed to Mom and told Joel *that's* who he needed to be interviewing!

THEN THE DREAM MORPHED TO ME WATCHING HOME VIDEOS. LOTS OF my childhood friends and classmates were in this dream. Mrs. Ray Mosley was sitting on a couch. A bunch of friends were on this sectional couch with her—Kendall Mosley, Danielle Lewis, Fran Lewis, Boose, Keith Stewart . . . Everyone was so young and having the best time. So much happiness and laughter in that video.

SLEEP DREAMS ARE OFTEN TIMES LIKE LIFE DREAMS—THEY DON'T HAVE to be spectacular to be special, and not everyone will get them. Still yet, no one has the right to minimize them if they bring an ounce of happiness to someone else.

81

KIM, ME, THE STOLEN DOG & THE TEA PARTY

October 25, 2019

I dreamed that my sister and I stole a dog from Hurricane. We had gone to investigate a house that was being built where Bonnie and Robert used to live. We were looking it over good from the car window when this vicious looking black dog popped up, Cujo style. It scared us to death! We rolled up the windows real quick and headed on up the holler.

As we rounded the curve at Farris Burton's house, I pointed up on the hill at the Big House that sat where Glenna Lou's house is. No idea why the Big House was up there, but I commented to Amanda how much I loved the Big House.

She was in the car for 2.7 seconds.

When we got back to Richmond, the dog popped out of the back seat wagging its tail, panting, and acting like it had had the best car ride of its life.

We didn't mean to steal the dog, so we took it back.

AFTER RETURNING THE NOT SO VICIOUS DOG, WE MADE A STOP ON Hurts Creek to unload someone's dishwasher. The dishwasher was in the curve across from Hurts Creek church. Just sitting out all by itself. Not plugged in. No water source. Nothing.

SIDE NOTE: I OFTEN DREAM ABOUT THESE HOUSES FARTHER OUT FROM the parking lot of the church. It's always two little brown wood shacks. A whole slew of little girls live in these houses that I've never seen before in my life. But they exist in my dreams.

ANYWAY, AS KIM AND I UNLOADED THIS DISHWASHER THAT WAS HOOKED to absolutely nothing, we pulled out teacup after teacup—most with Easter themes, bunnies, eggs, various pastels . . . The little girls in the shacks had had a tea party.

IT NEVER OCCURRED TO US WHAT WE'D DO WITH THE DISHES ONCE WE unloaded them. Or how they couldn't possibly be clean. *Or* even why we thought it was our job or our business to unload their dishwasher.

BUT, AS THE DREAM ENDED, WE DUTIFULLY EXAMINED THE PETER RABBIT cups on the bottom rack . . . which didn't fit the era of the little girls at all. And neither did an automatic dishwasher.

I HAD GONE SO LONG WITHOUT REMEMBERING MY DREAMS. MY DREAM people have amped the heck back up! They wear me out!

82

BUTCHER HOLLER, ME & THE POWDER BLUE VACUUM CLEANER

November 04, 2019

I dreamt I was driving a powder blue, Electrolux canister vacuum up Butcher Holler.

Loretta couldn't dream of leaving Butcher Holler, and I—apparently—was hellbent!

** This dream came the night that Bru and I actually went to Butcher Holler, In Van Lear, Kentucky, to see Loretta Lynn's cabin.

I was so excited to go. However, once we got there, we realized that no one was at the house to show us around.

Moral to the story: *Always* call ahead to assure that the days and hours of operation coincide with your trip.

83

LITTLE AMY OAKLEY

November 07, 2019

I dreamed that I was away from home when our alarm system sent a notification that someone was breaking in. I called 911 and met the officer at the house. No perpetrator.

I went back to where I was when I got the notification again.

This time, I didn't call for help.

I showed up at the house, eased through the kitchen, backed up against the wall so he couldn't see me, and whirled around to peek out the window. There were two of them.

I cocked my shotgun with one hand, burst through the door,

and pistol whipped him with *both* ends of the shotgun. I was just finishing up with the first guy—not having had a fair crack at the other—when I woke up.

I don't know what this means, but you probably shouldn't test your luck!

84

BOOSE, ME, THE SHOTGUNS & BACON

November 10, 2019

To my cousin, Boose: I dreamed about you.

We were about to mess somebody up.

There was some man who had done you wrong. You had called him and lured him to the house—never seen this house before in my life.

It was basically vacant.

We had these shotguns loaded and waiting, about fifteen of them were laid out on this cabinet.

. . .

We were bad. But we were also crazy. On the end of each gun, we had a strip of bacon attached. Guess we were also hangry.

We were sitting on a bed in the living room. The head of the bed was between two windows that backed up to the driveway.

We were sitting there waiting when you said that you had to go to the store. I jumped up and protested. But I actually think my protest was because I was afraid I'd fall asleep and miss him showing up.

You grabbed a book off the shelf of the headboard and said, "Here. Read this!"

I looked at you like you were crazy and said, "I can't concentrate on this knowing what we are about to do!"

I never once thought it was a bad idea.

As the dream ended, his big heavy boots had just scrapped across the porch. He was at the door . . .

85

CAINT A GIRL JUST GET SOME COLOR?

November 19, 2019

The other night, I dreamt about my friend, Christa Jordan Aubrey. I dreamed I was in this huge house. Castle like. *Apparently,* I wasn't allowed in this certain room. The guards came to drag me away just as I spotted her.

I grasped the doorframe with my fingertips and clutched it until they dragged me away—my fingertips releasing the frame, one by one as they pulled me away. The whole time, I was screaming out to her, "ASK LAUREN ABOUT OVERTONES!" (Her daughter is a cosmetologist.)

Apparently, I'm in desperate need of highlights, and my subconscious thinks that Lauren is just the girl for the job!

86

CRYING LIKE A BABY

December 08, 2019

I dreamed I was pregnant with six babies. I woke up crying. I can't swear those were tears of joy!

I need to take to my bed now.

87

THE NAUGHTY LIST, PORCH JAIL & THE CASHIER

December 28, 2019

Children, I had a wild night of dreams! I dreamed I had found myself on Santa's Naughty List. I had five offenses, but I can only remember one. My top charge was cussing.

We were imprisoned on my Granny's porch until we worked off our misdeeds.

I cussed Santa like a sailor when I realized that naughty list was a real thing, and I was in jail over it. That little stint earned me even more time in the porch pokey.

I'd wrack up more offenses when I'd try to tell people what they were doing wrong and when I'd try to stop them when I knew they'd get in trouble.

. . .

ONE DAY, SANTA HAD HIS LIST OUT, SO I STROLLED BY HIS DESK—SUPER slow—trying to see how many offenses I still had. I had one. *One*. I was almost out! Then I had the thought that looking at the list was probably an offense, so I went to the corner and cried. I guess the old guy liked me by then because he came over and assured me that looking at my own list wasn't an extra charge—I guess since I was only worrying about myself.

ODDLY, THAT PORCH JAIL TAUGHT ME THAT PEOPLE HAVE TO CHANGE ON their own, that no amount of showing them what they're doing wrong will help, and no amount of trying to stop them will actually make them stop.

EXCEPT ME, WHO HAD TO LEARN THIS IN PORCH JAIL ON MY GRANNY'S porch for being on Santa's naughty list.

SHITE! I THINK THAT PORCH JAIL REPRESENTED MATURITY.

THEN THE DREAM MORPHED TO KIM AND ME BEING AT THE STORE, which was actually the high school. She saw all these toys piled up and inquired about them.

THE STORE WAS TRYING TO GET PEOPLE TO TAKE THEM FOR CHARITY. The clerk said we had three ways of doing this. He said we could take them with no strings attached, sell them for thirty cents and keep the money, or take them, sell them for thirty cents, *and* give the money to charity.

. . .

WELL, IF PORCH JAIL TAUGHT ME ANYTHING, YOU DON'T GO THE EASY route because you *will* end up on Santa's Naughty List!

SO OFF TO MEIJER I WENT—WHICH WAS ACTUALLY MAGIC MART IN Hazard.

THEY PUT ME ON A REGISTER RIGHT AWAY, AND EIGHT MILLION PEOPLE got in my line with ten million things each.

THEY WERE ALL ANGRY AND ALL IN A HURRY.

MY FIRST CUSTOMER TRIED TO CASH A PAYCHECK. I KEPT TRYING TO scan it and finally shouted, "I don't know how to do this!"

SHE STORMED OFF ANGRY.

THERE WERE THREE CASHIERS STANDING BY TO HELP ME, BUT NO ONE was very helpful. The two women just looked at me, and the man kept screaming at me to use the "In a hurry" button. "Inahurry." One word. It also gave a 10% discount.

MY LITTLE ANGRY WOMAN CUSTOMER WAS THE ANGRIEST OF ALL. SHE also had the most stuff of all, including stuff they didn't typically sell. I charged her $616 for a roast. She nearly had a coronary.

DURING THIS TIME, BRU CAME TO ME AND SHOWED ME A RECEIPT FOR his purchase that he'd made on the other side of the store. Even my husband chose a different cashier! They had undercharged him. Santa jail came back to me, and I screamed at the top of my lungs, "Go back, and tell them they undercharged you!" Everyone thought I was crazy, but an ex-con knows how to walk the line. And you never know when Santa is watching.

Customer after customer came through my line. Everyone wanted to talk to me. I thought it would be handy if you had one person to ring up the purchases, one to talk to the customers, and another to bag the groceries. I just couldn't do it all. And they *all* wanted to talk! *A lot*!

Sometimes I'd remember to ask if they wanted a toy, but most times I didn't. And every time I did ask, they'd say no.

That is, until Michael Johnson came through my line. He bought a toy. Even after I said, "It's literally only one dime and one nickel! I mean, two dimes and one nickel. Sigh. IT's TWO DIMES AND TWO NICKLES. OK?" Bless it. He still bought one after that pitiful spiel.

In the end, I gave no one their receipt. My unhelpful female helpers took great pleasure in going through my mile long receipt and marking a line in pencil after every customer total. One would mark it; the other would lop it off with giant silver scissors.

At the end of the day, I was *tard*, like Lorettie. I give mad props to anyone who works retail. I'm still exhausted after my shift! People are not nice. And they talk too much. And they are absolutely always angry and in a hurry.

I'll leave you with this, the Naughty List is a real thing. Be nice to your cashiers, and be quiet. And be good, for goodness' sake!

I'll be back in porch jail for tellin' y'all this. And for not giving that thirty cents to the charity those toys came from.

88

THE BRADY BUNCH HOUSE, SHAQUILLE O'NEAL, AND THAT TIME I WENT TO PRISON

January 17, 2020

I dreamed I was in Uncle Dave and Aunt Helen's old house on the Spur.

Suddenly, the house morphed into the Brady House from the Brady Bunch. And, apparently, we used to live there.

The house had been sold, and the producers were forcing me to leave.

Before I did, I was gonna sing one more song because it had been my daddy's favorite. No clue what the song was, but I was giving it my absolute all.

All of a sudden, these mobster people burst in. They had come for my co-worker who was still inside. My coworker was Shaquille O'Neal. These people were little peons, so I don't know how they drug him out.

I SHOT THEM BOTH, BUT THEY KEPT RIGHT ON PULLING HIM OUT OF THE house.

THEN THE DREAM MORPHED AGAIN. TIME HAD PASSED. I'M GUESSING I had been in jail. Anyway, Kim, Mom, Mammaw, and I told these people that we were going to the restaurant. We said it super loud so everyone would hear. Everyone. Like in the next town, even.

WE PILED IN OUR CAR, THE BRADY STATION WAGON, AND I TOLD THEM we were taking a detour.

I DROVE LIKE A MADWOMAN DOWN THOSE DESOLATE STREETS. THEY looked more like a war torn third world country than a bustling American street.

ANYWAY, I DROVE THIS CAR LIKE I STOLE IT—BECAUSE I LIKELY HAD.

WE PULLED UP ON THIS RIDGE AND HAD TO TRY TO GET DOWN TO THE house. Mammaw and Mom were troopers because they propelled right down that mountainside like it was an everyday occurrence.

SO WE GOT INSIDE THIS HOUSE AND FOUND A BUNCH OF ROOMS THAT

had sets straight out of the show. There was a set that had the Brady's backyard, playground, those little egg looking seats, their dining room table . . .

I REALIZED THAT MIKE AND CAROL REALLY DID HAVE SEPARATE bedrooms, and they were on opposite ends of this house.

THIS WASN'T A MOVIE STUDIO. IT WAS AN ACTUAL HOUSE. AND YOU could've fit about five of those TV houses inside this dream house. It was enormous.

MIKE BRADY HAD A FIREPLACE IN HIS DEN. HIS DEN WAS ABOUT THE SIZE of my house, and the fireplace opening was as tall as him. It was ginormous.

ANYWAY, I GOT SEPARATED FROM MOM, MAMMAW, AND KIM.

AS I MEANDERED ABOUT THE HOUSE, I OVERHEARD THAT THE HOUSE WAS slated to be torn down.

I found a staff member, explained I used to live there, and talked her into getting me into private sets.

I didn't have a phone. I guess we hadn't been issued those in prison, so I hadn't acquired one yet.

I talked her into letting me use her phone. I took picture after picture in our rushed tour. I was worried she wouldn't actually send me the pictures when we were done, but I didn't know anyone's number to send them myself.

She took me to sets I'd never even seen on tv—one of which was an upstairs den that I've dreamed of before.

I mean, it wasn't Mike Brady's den in the other dreams. Sometimes it's a bedroom. But I usually wake up before I make it inside. I'm usually climbing three billon windy steps to get there.

But I digress.

Back to this dream . . .

We kept taking elevators to floor after floor of hidden sets. One set had a wind tunnel on it. A man and woman suited up, goggles and all, and harnessed themselves in. We took pictures of them and just had a big time. When it was time for the staff member and me to suit up and the couple to take our pictures, as we were stepping into this apparatus, the man squealed on us, which sent people scrambling after us.

We got away, and I broke away from the staff member. Come to think of it, I don't even know why she was running . . .

Anyway, I was bound and determined to make it to that room where I used to sing with my daddy. I wanted the sheet music. Because, apparently, we were professional about our melodies.

I never made it to the room in the far corner, but I did a lot of running, hiding, and petty theft along the way.

I passed this room that had a big rectangular chest on the floor. It was the only furniture in the room. All these people were huddled around the chest, filling their pockets full. That made me mad as a wet hen because that was my brother's stuff, so I burst into the room, screaming, shouting, and putting the fear of God into them.

IT WORKED IN THE SENSE THAT THEY STOPPED WHAT THEY WERE DOING, but the higher ups had now been alerted to my presence.

I TOOK OFF RUNNING.

I ENDED UP WITH MOM, MAMMAW, AND KIM AGAIN. WE WERE WALKING down a ramp, and I was trying to shield my face so the other people didn't recognize me.

IT WAS IN THIS MOMENT THAT I PASSED SHAQUILLE O'NEAL *LIAR* PANTS. He hadn't been carted off by the mob. He was working with them to get my house!

HE WAS WEARING A PLAIN GRAY SWEATSUIT—ONE THAT EVEN I COULD afford. If the Dollar Tree sold clothes, this would have been it.

He looked awful. Well, it was his hair that made him look awful. Hair. He had some, and it was dirty gray from plaster falling in it.

I WAS MAD ALL OVER AGAIN BECAUSE I WENT TO PRISON TRYING TO protect him!

I SCREAMED OUT, "HEY!"

. . .

All eyes swept to me.

And just like that, I was on the run again . . .

89

PAVE YOUR OWN WAY

January 18, 2020

I dreamed that Tyler and I piled in the car. I was driving.

We headed down the road. When I got ready to merge onto the interstate, I glanced over at him. He was terrified. I asked him what was wrong.

He said, "The last time we did this, Dad was sick."

I glanced in the backseat. Sure enough, Bru was sitting back there, sick and scared. And in the fetal position.

Bless it.

Anyway, I merged onto the interstate . . .

. . .

IN DOING SO, I NOTICED SOME PECULIARITIES ABOUT THIS ROAD.

The land itself was wide—as wide as both north and southbound lanes typically would be. What was interesting about this gigantic road was that it appeared to be a one way interstate.

The other fascinating thing about this road is that it wasn't a road at all. There was no pavement anywhere. It was covered in grass. My road was basically a field.

There were no cars ahead of me, and if there were any behind me, I didn't notice them. I wasn't looking that way for long.

My car moved from side to side like a race car trying to make its way into the lead spot. I wasn't moving past anything. I was just weaving in that erratic manner because I could.

As I moved along my organic highway, I noticed a curious amenity to my car: it was also a lawnmower.

So, as I wound my way about the road, I laid the path for those who would follow.

As I zigzagged across that wide open interstate, I mowed grass all the way to London.

KINDA FELT LIKE I NEEDED A LOW PONYTAIL, TAILORED BRITCHES, AND knee boots. I was like a founding father cutting a path through that tract of land. Or maybe I needed a coonskin cap like Daniel Boone because I was a trailblazer. Or *maybe*—Ok, I'll stop right there. But I was about to quote Captain Kirk . . .

Whatever we call it, I was important because I was doing something that had never been done before.

WHICH BRINGS ME TO THIS THOUGHT AND A PERFECT STOPPING POINT for my book—regardless of which hat I wear, I'm glad I chose the one of writer and decided to publish this book of crazy dreams. If even one person got a laugh or single moment of reprieve from it, it was well worth it.

. . .

I hope you've enjoyed My Crazy Dreams.

~ Amy

A NOTE FROM THE AUTHOR

Thank you for your purchase. If you enjoyed My Crazy Dreams, please consider leaving a review. It doesn't have to be anything elaborate, just a few words. You could even say something about your favorite chapter or simply state the chapter title. It would be interesting to read which entries connected most with readers.

Reviews help encourage others to take a closer look at an author's work. They're appreciated more than you know.

ACKNOWLEDGMENTS

To my cousin, Anne Kilburn, thank you for the years of encouragement to publish my dreams. It has been a lot of fun to go back and compile them.

To my friend, Robin Garrison, thanks for your help. It's been so long, you probably don't even remember it, but I do. I appreciate you, girl.

To all my other friends and family who have encouraged me over the years to write this book, it's been a long time coming, but I hope you've enjoyed it.

ABOUT THE AUTHOR

Amy Pennington Brudnicki was born and raised in Hyden, a quaint town in southeastern Kentucky. At an early age, she penned clandestine paranormal mysteries—nothing more than a page in length and always quickly discarded. As a forlorn teen, she began to write poetry. Her collection was stored in a ratty old notebook and tucked away out of sight.

Throughout her life, she wrote tales that would evoke laughter in anyone who read them. Of course, this was all before the age of internet. Shortly after high school, Amy's home was destroyed by fire. She and her family lost everything they had, stories and poems included.

Thinking that writing was nothing more than a hobby, she laid her pen aside and focused on her education and starting a family.

Years later, her old soul caught up with her as she felt that familiar pull once more. She has since written countless stories of non-fiction, reflective articles, a romantic suspense novel, guided journals to preserve family history, a collection of short stories about her Kentucky life, and this book of her crazy dreams.

Her purpose in sharing this with you is to urge you not to give up on *your* dreams. She'd tell you that it's never too late to dream a new dream, just as it's never too late to explore one previously set aside.

In the powerful words of Aerosmith, "Dream on. Dream on. Dream until your dreams come true."

facebook.com/amybru

ALSO BY AMY: AMY USES A VARIETY OF PEN NAMES WHEN SHE WRITES OTHER GENRES—AMELIA BLAKE IS HER PSEUDONYM WHEN SHE WRITES FICTION, AND OLD SOUL PUBLICATIONS IS THE AUTHOR NAME FOR HER GUIDED JOURNALS. THE SOLE PURPOSE OF THIS IS TO DIFFERENTIATE BETWEEN WRITING STYLES. MY LEGACY BY OLD SOUL PUBLICATIONS IS A GUIDED QUESTIONNAIRE JOURNAL TO HELP PRESERVE FAMILY HISTORY. VANISHED BY AMELIA BLAKE IS A STEAMY, ROMANTIC SUSPENSE. AND ECHOES OF THE PAST: MY DIRT ROAD DIARY IS A COLLECTION OF SHORT STORIES ABOUT AMY'S KENTUCKY LIFE.

(1) Echoes of the Past: My Dirt Road Diary by Amy Pennington Brudnicki

(2) Vanished by Amelia Blake

(3) My Legacy by Old Soul Publications